So let's go on a **LIFESIZE** adventure,
and see how you measure up against some
of the world's most amazing animals...

Here is a **LIFESIZE** bee hummingbird – isn't it tiny?
In fact, it's the world's smallest bird and it can beat
its wings a super speedy 80 times a second.
Try flapping your arms that fast!

High-five a polar bear! Put your paw
on the polar bear's **LIFESIZE**
paw – whose is the biggest?

Polar bears live in a place called the Arctic, which is rather chilly! BRRRRRR! HUGE paws help spread their weight on the snow and ice.

Who else lives here?

A narwhal's tusk is actually a tooth that grows through its top lip. Ouch! It can be up to 3 metres long.

These **LIFESIZE** lampreys have 11 to 12 rows of teeth. That's a lot of brushing before bedtime!

Try on a **LIFESIZE** toco toucan's beak. Hold it up to the side of your nose. How does it look?

The **toco toucan** lives in the hot, leafy forests of Cuba. Its super-snazzy beak makes up one third of its total size. That's like you having a beak that's half as tall as you are!

What other birds live in Cuba's forests?

Cuban parakeets are really sociable. This **LIFESIZE** parakeet is enjoying the shade and looking for some parakeet friends to play with.

Look! A flamboyance of flamingoes!

Aren't these **LIFESIZE** todies pretty? Their bright feathers aren't just for show, they are for camouflage in the colourful Cuban forests.

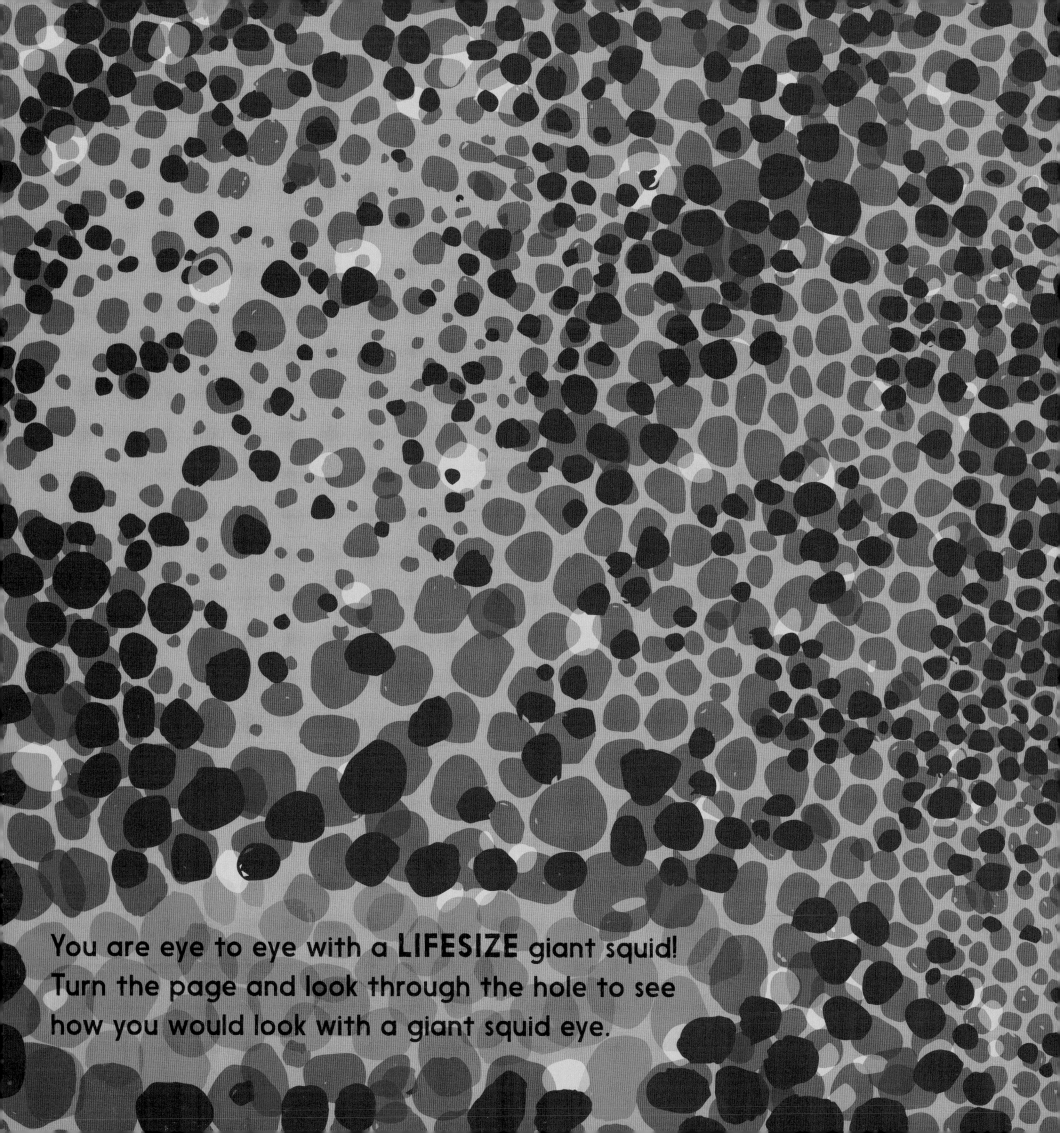

You are eye to eye with a **LIFESIZE** giant squid!
Turn the page and look through the hole to see
how you would look with a giant squid eye.

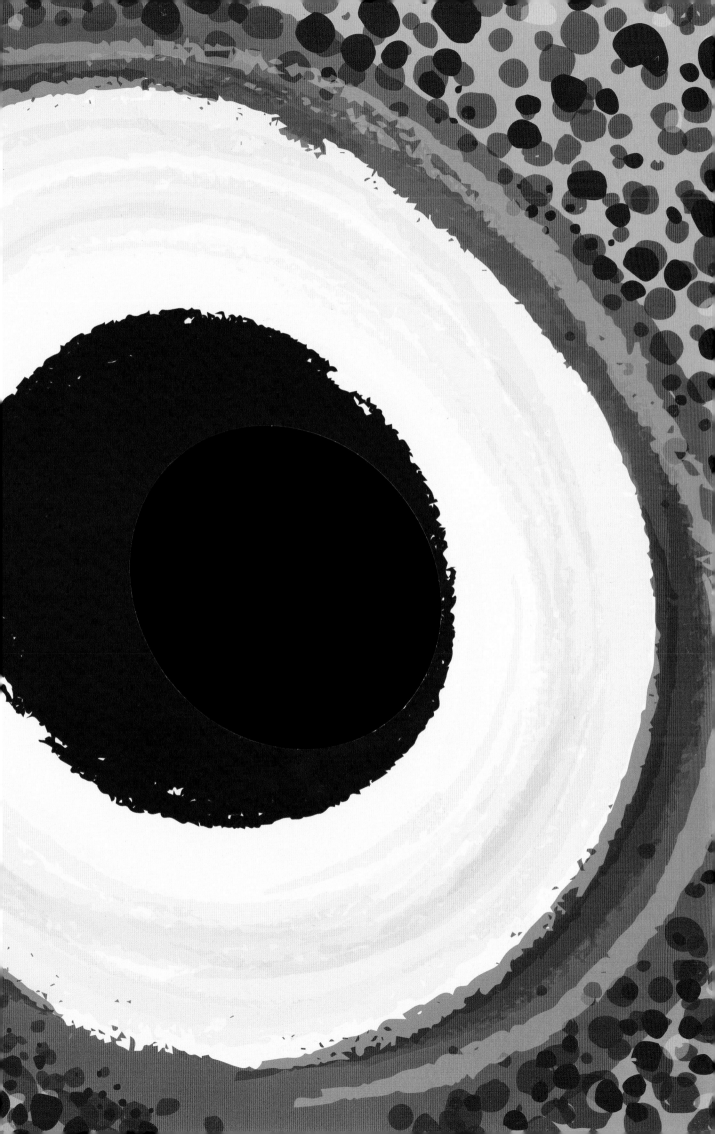

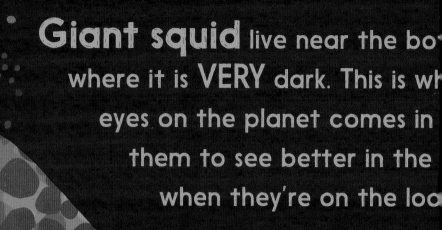

Giant squid live near the bo[ttom] where it is VERY dark. This is wh[y] eyes on the planet comes in [handy] them to see better in the [dark] when they're on the loo[kout]

Who else lives dow[n here?]

Irukandji jellyfish are the smallest jellyfish in the world. They glow in the dark, just like the giant squid. But don't let the tiny twinkliness of this **LIFESIZE** jellyfish fool you, it has a powerful sting!

This **LIFESIZE** pea crab
is tiny! Although he is only
six millimetres wide, he has 10 legs.
That's eight more than you!

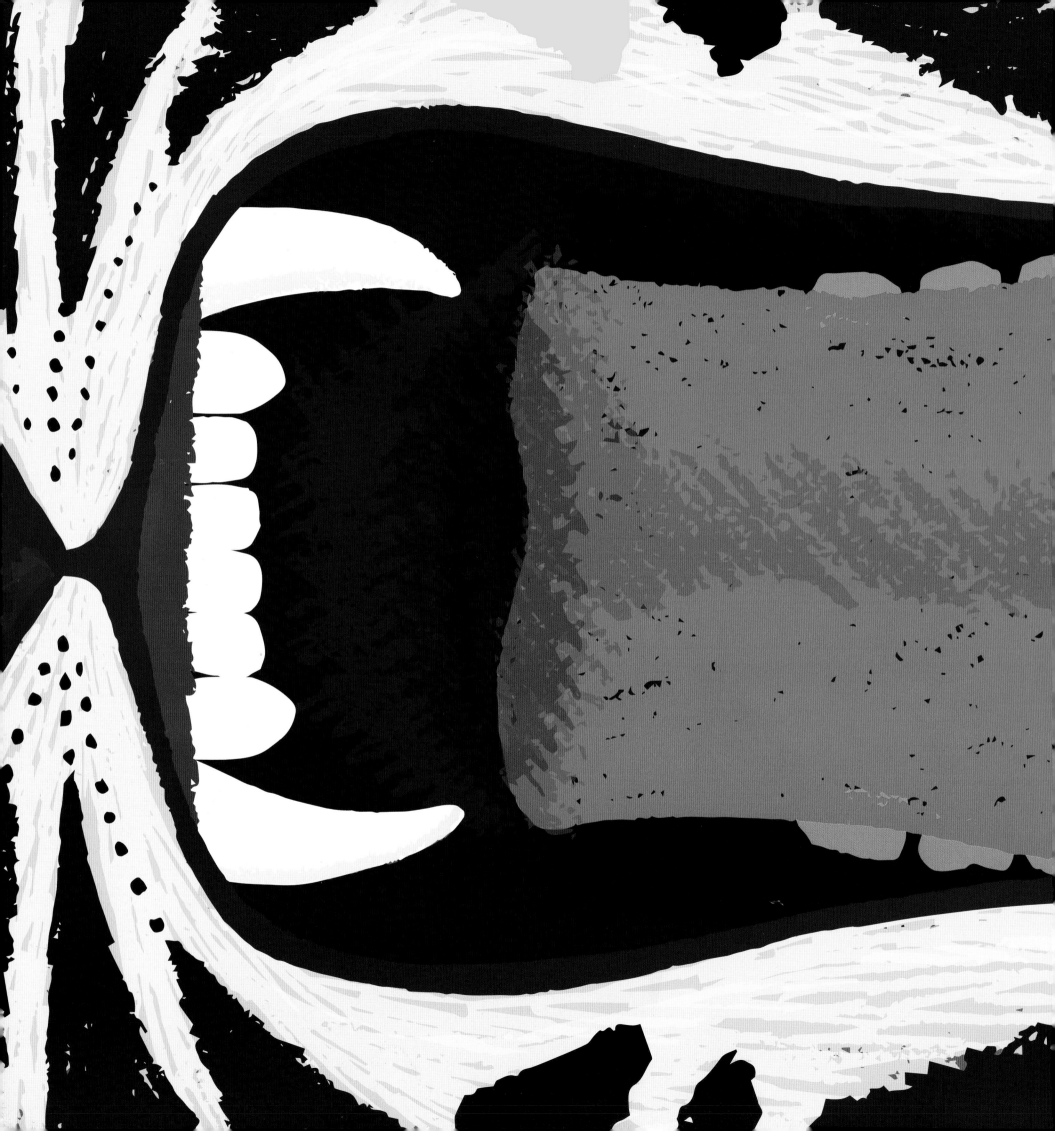

ROOOAAAARRR like a Bengal tiger! Hold the book under your nose to see what you would look like with a LIFESIZE tiger roar.

Most **Bengal tigers** live in the vast forests of India. But it's easy for them to stay in touch as their roars can be heard up to three kilometres away. Pardon?

What other animals can you spot?

This is a **LIFESIZE** tiger centipede. These creatures have so many legs that they are bound to lose one here or there. But don't worry, they can just grow another!

Grey langur monkeys and chital deer are great friends, warning each other if there are any predators coming. **LOOK OUT FOR THE TIGER!**

Here is a **LIFESIZE** leaf insect! These clever insects pretend to be leaves so they can hide from predators. Sneaky!

Stick your tongue out at a **LIFESIZE** giraffe!
Whose tongue is the longest?

African elephants are the largest land animals on the planet. They also have the biggest ears, which they flap about to keep cool.

Cheetahs are completely dotty. No really, they each have up to 3,000 spots!

Giraffes live on the hot, grassy plains of Africa. They are the world's TALLEST animal so it makes sense they have an extraordinarily long tongue. This helps them reach the leaves on acacia trees. Yum!

What other animals live here?

This **LIFESIZE** male rainbow lizard is usually reddish-brown but it turns rainbow coloured to impress lady lizards.

Try these **LIFESIZE** kangaroo ears on for size.
Hold them up to your forehead and jump about
a bit. You are practically a kangaroo!

The fancy frill-necked lizard opens its mouth and pushes out its frill to scare away other animals. Boo!

Red kangaroos live in the hot and dusty Australian outback. Their big, pointy ears can swivel to pick up sounds from all around.

What other creatures live here?

To get out of the hot sun, this **LIFESIZE** desert scorpion can burrow up to one metre down in a twirly spiral. Phew!

Giant squid

Tentacle tip to tail: up to 18 metres

Did you know? A giant squid has eight arms and two tentacles. If a giant squid loses a arm, it just grows another one.

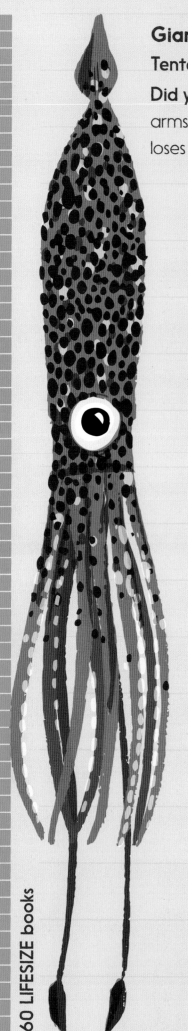

60 LIFESIZE books

Wow! We've travelled the world and seen some amazing **LIFESIZE** animals. Let's see how these animals compare in size to one another.

Giraffe

Head to toe: up to 5.5 metres

Did you know? A group of giraffes is called a tower.

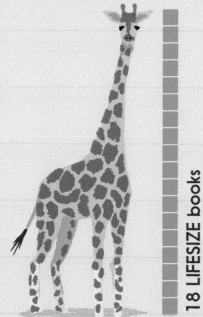

18 LIFESIZE books

African elephant

Head to toe: up to 4 metres

Did you know? Elephant tusks are extra long front (incisor) teeth.

13 LIFESIZE books

Bengal tiger

Head to tail: up to 2.7 metres

Did you know? Every tiger has its own unique stripes – no two tigers are the same!

9 LIFESIZE books

2 LIFESIZE books

Toco toucan

Beak to tail: up to 63 centimetres
The beak alone is 19 centimetres!

Did you know? Toucans rest their beaks
on their backs when they sleep.

**Where do you fit into the line-up?
Measure yourself using this book to
see how you compare. Are you utterly
GIGANTIC** or teeny tiny? **Try measuring
your friends and family as well!**

Bee hummingbird

Head to tail: up to 6 centimetres

Did you know? Hummingbirds lick
sweet nectar out of flowers and
can lick up to 13 times a second!

Polar bear

Head to tail: up to 2.5 metres

Did you know? Polar bears have
an amazing sense of smell and can
smell prey up to 16 kilometres away.

Red kangaroo

Head to toe: up to 1.5 metres

Did you know? A male is called
a boomer, a female is called a
flyer and a baby is called a joey.

Giant panda

Head to tail: up to 1.5 metres

Did you know? Pandas spend up
to 12 hours eating every day.

8 LIFESIZE books

5 LIFESIZE books

5 LIFESIZE books